1

**Synopsis of the True Story of The Airship Flap and UFOs' sightings of 1896-1897**

From the Series
Ufology's Most Important Topics.

\*\*\*   \*\*\*   \*\*\*

# Maximillien de Lafayette

## SYNOPSIS OF THE TRUE STORY OF THE GREAT AIRSHIP FLAP AND UFOs SIGHTINGS OF 1896-1897

**From the Series**
Ufology's Most Important Topics.

Published in the United States of America and Germany.

Printed by Times Square Press. New York.
Date of Publication: July 23, 2014.

**Synopsis of the True Story of the Great Airship Flap and UFOs' sightings of 1896-1897**

From the Series
Ufology's Most Important Topics.

# Maximillien de Lafayette

\*\*\* \*\*\* \*\*\*

Times Square Press
New York  Berlin  Paris  Madrid
2014

# Table Of Contents

\*\*\* \*\*\* \*\*\*

# The Full Story of the Great Airship Flap of the 1896-1897

Even though, avalanches of pieces of evidence, hundreds upon hundreds of irrefutable documents, and mountains of historical and scientific findings which demonstrated without the shadow of a doubt, that the unidentified flying crafts and UFOs' sightings of 1896-1897 had nothing to do with aliens, and extraterrestrial flying saucers, ufologists and ufology's enthusiasts still believe that what flew over American cities during the Great Airship Flap were aliens' UFOs! They are absolutely wrong!!

**Here is the full story:**
The first sighting of a single luminous flying saucer occurred on October 26, 1896, in San Francisco, California, as reported by a local resident.
On November 1, 1896, a man reported seeing an airship over Bolinas Ridge.
On November 17, 1896, many local residents reported a huge bright light moving in the sky, and flying at an approximate altitude of 300-400 feet.
It was beaming some sort of a light coming from under its belly. Some witnesses, even stated, that they saw people inside a dome on the top of the airship.
It appeared to them as if they were directing the flying object.
On November 20, 1896, several flying objects in the sky of Oakland, California were seen by thousands of witnesses. Many witnesses reported seeing different kinds of crafts on the ground with crew repairing the airships.

For the next three days, more flying objects with a visible round cockpit with people inside were spotted in various parts of California.

A businessman and a former attorney general of the State of California, who became extremely interested in these sightings, told the media and the public that those flying objects were airships invented by a man who works for General Marco, then the commander-in-chief of the national military forces in Cuba.

Many believed that the attorney general's story was a cover-up. Even back then, conspiracies and cover-ups seemed to be part of official procedures, but what is very distinct and different from nowadays cover-ups, is the fact that the 1896's cover-up was not of a military or a governmental nature, but rather of a secretive business and entrepreneurial nature, as investigative discoveries and findings would later suggest.
Many embellished stories and fabrications began to circulate, and some leading newspapers fueled the curiosity of the public.

But everything changed, when the airships, all of a sudden began to appear all over the country by March 1897, and especially on April 1, 1897, when a huge luminous airship, thirty foot long, displayed an astonishing flight pattern in the sky of Kansas City, which was witnessed by thousands of people, and reported by the New York Sun newspaper on April 3, 1897.

*** *** ***

Artist's illustration of an airship of the era. Published by the
Saint Paul Globe, Minnesota in 1897.
Many witnesses reported seeing such airships with highly visible
wings.

Artist's illustration of one of the airships that appeared over California, and published by the San Francisco Call newspaper, on November 22, 1896.

---

### Different shapes of flying objects:

One judge in Texas claimed that he spoke to a crew of a two hundred foot long airship who told him that they came from the North Pole and were en route around the world.

Illustration of the era.
It is clearly a "Dirigible", and not an alien UFO!

———————————————————————

Several witnesses from Wisconsin, Iowa, Kansas, and California described the mystery airship as a long metallic cigar flying at a low altitude.

While other witnesses stated that the airship was round like a balloon with a shiny metallic body. A third group reported that the airship had the shape of a cigar which lifted a rectangular compartment underneath.

The compartment which looked like a cabin was well-lit, and a crew of three people was seen inside the dome maneuvering the craft. The different versions of the shape, speed and altitude of the flying object led observers and concerned investigators to believe that there were more than one airship in the area, especially when latest sighting's reports described the object as a round airship with huge dome (cockpit) attached to two wings on both side of the airship.

It got more interesting, and perhaps more complicated when numerous witnesses reported that the crew of the airship was beaming some sort of light over houses and particular areas on the ground.

The varied versions of the description of the mysterious flying objects were published in the Chicago Tribune, the New York Sun, the Chicago Times, the New York Herald, and the New York Times.

The New York Times published 3 photos of the airship, and other newspapers sketched the flying object according to eye witnesses' reports.

*** *** ***

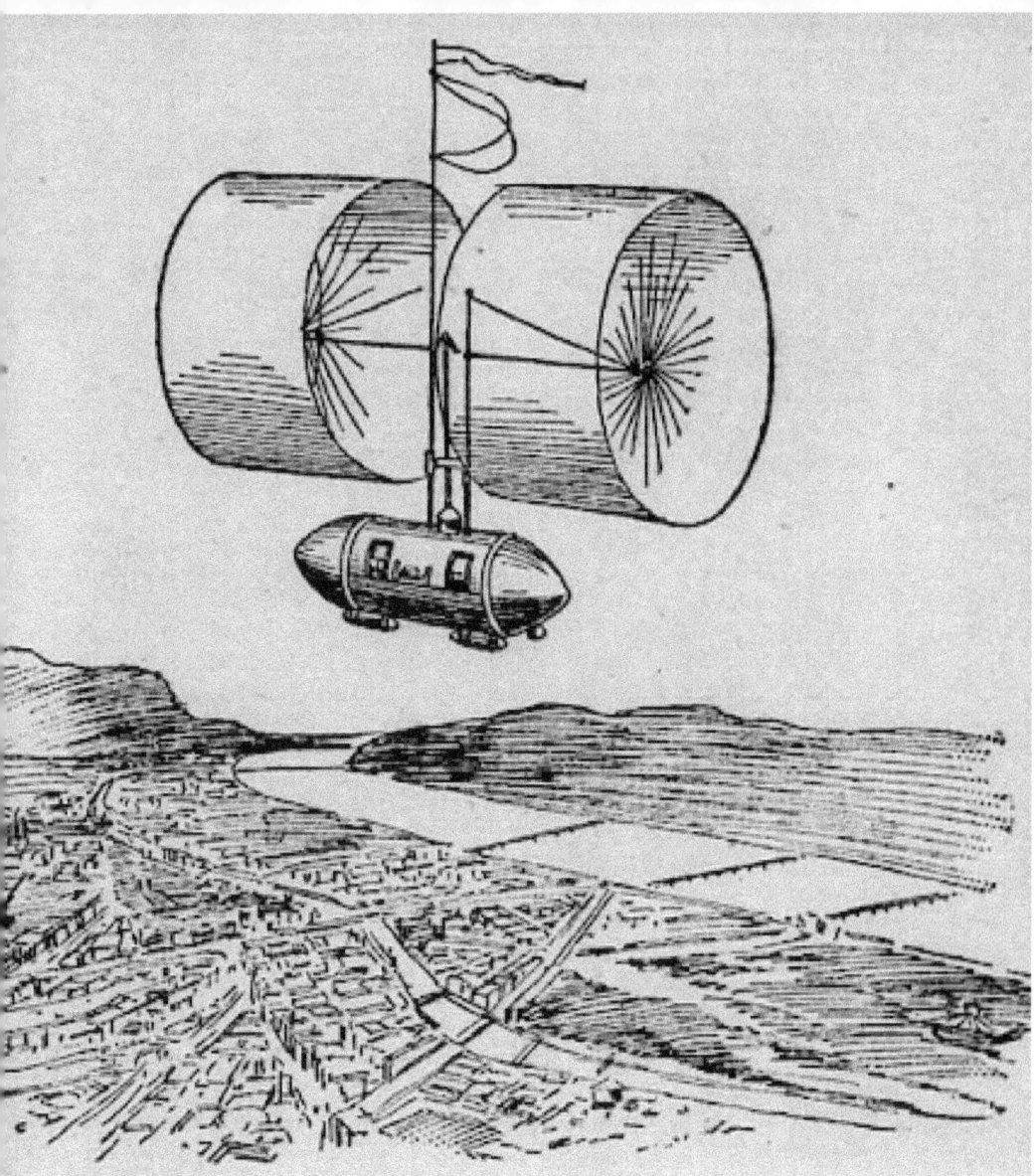

1897 Wellner's airship.

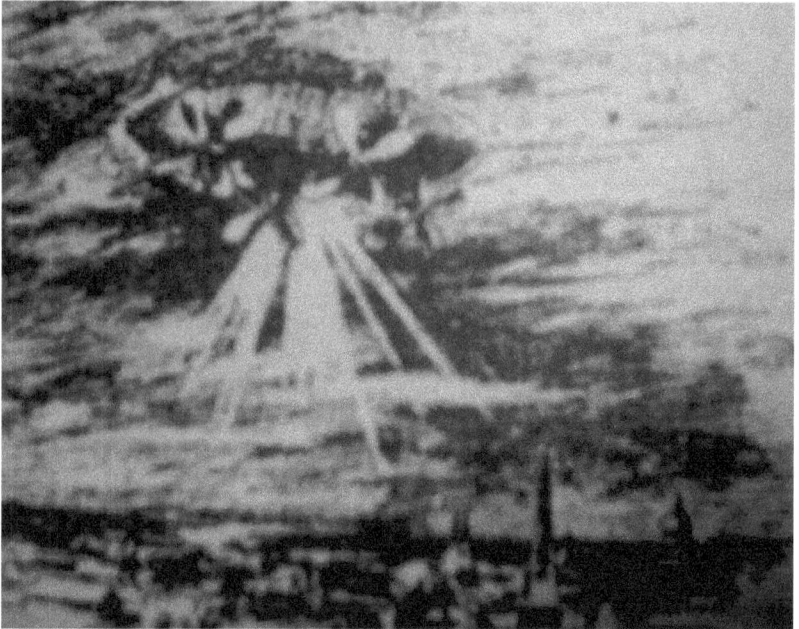

Airship over Sacramento, California, in 1896, as published by the San Francisco Call.

Articles in the papers of the era mentioned John W. Keely's airship which he built and kept on developing between 1888 and 1893. The airship flew successfully and was acknowledged by the United States War Department in 1896.

By now, everybody has heard of the mysterious flying objects.

**Press clippings:**
On April 12, 1897, the Chicago Tribune published the following, and contributed to Max L. Harmar, the Secretary of the Chicago Aeronautical Society, "One person knows all about the airship. He says: These thousands of people didn't see a steel hull because this is the airship my friend built in California and is on its way here to Chicago."
On April 2, 1897, the Chicago Record reported, "Missouri people excited: Mystical black object casting before it red light startled whole city for the last two weeks!

An artist illustration of an airship over Chicago published by the Chicago Times-Herald, on April 12, 1897.

Ten thousand people swear they have no hallucinations! Scoffers and disbelievers claim the people have been seeing the planet Venus or the Evening Star, even though according to the almanac this planet should have set below the horizon at least an hour before!

Object appeared very swiftly, then appeared to stop and hover over the city for ten minutes at a time, then after flashing its green-blue and white lights, shot upwards into space....light gradually twinkling away and looking like a bright star."

On December 1, 1896,  the Oakland Tribune newspaper reported that an airship was seen over Oakland, California, on November 26, and a witness described the object as a big black cigar...it was100 feet in length, and a triangular tail was attached to it.

It appeared that the main body of the airship was made of aluminum. It flew at a tremendous speed.

Deputy Sheriff John McLemore of Garland County, and Constable John Sumpter Jr. stated that on the night of May 6, 1897, they noticed a brilliant light in the sky, and later saw two persons moving around the airship carrying lanterns. One of the men approached them and told them that he and two other persons were traveling around the country in an airship.

 The Deputy Sheriff and the Constable described the airship as a cigar-shaped airship, sixty feet in length, similar to those the newspapers wrote about.

On May 13, 1897, the Arkansas Weekly World paper wrote, a man was filling a sack with water and a woman was standing in the dark. The paper stated, word for word, "The man with the whiskers invited us to take a ride, saying that he could take us where it was not raining."

"We told him we preferred to get wet."

"Asking the man why the brilliant light was turned on and off so much, he replied that the light was so powerful that it consumed a great deal of his motive power. He said he would like to stop off in Hot Springs for a few days and take the hot baths, but his time was limited and he could not. He said they were going to wind up at Nashville, Tennessee, after thoroughly seeing the country."

Artist's illustration of one of the airships that appeared over California, and published by the Oakland Tribune and other San Francisco newspapers, in 1897.

Artist's illustration of the era of an airship over Arkansas, 1897.

On April 26, 1896, The Houston Daily Post, Merkel, Texas, published the following article: "Some parties returning from church last night noticed a heavy object dragging along with a rope attached.

They followed it until in crossing the railroad it caught on a rail. On looking up they saw what they supposed was the airship.

It was not near enough to get an idea of the dimensions.

A light could be seen protruding from several windows; one bright light in front like the headlight of a locomotive.

After some ten minutes a man was seen descending the rope; he came near enough to be plainly seen.

He wore a light blue sailor suit, was small in size. He stopped when he discovered parties at the anchor and cut the ropes below him and sailed off in a northeast direction.

\*\*\* \*\*\* \*\*\*

Artist's illustration of the mysterious airship of 1896-1897.

An airship landed in Iowa, 1987.

The anchor is now on exhibition at the blacksmith shop of Elliott and Miller and is attracting the attention of hundreds of people.

Des Moines Leader, April 11, 1897, reported that the residents of Waterloo, Iowa, found a 36-foot airship made from wood and canvas and fitted with generators compressors. The airship was directed by a large crew.

The "operators" of the craft told the residents of the area that they flew from San Francisco.

Testimonies and affidavits:
Alexander Hamilton, member of the House of Representative, E. W. Wharton, State Oil Inspector, M. E. H.unt, Sheriff, W. L.auber, Deputy Sheriff, H. H. Winter, Banker, H. S. Johnson, Pharmacist, J. H. Stitcher, Attorney, Alexander Stewart, Justice of the Peace, H. C. Rollins, Postmaster, and James W. Martin, Registrar of Deeds, signed an affidavit on April, 21, 1897, in which she stated (Excerpts), "We are awakened by a noise among the cattle.

I rose, thinking that perhaps my bulldog was performing some of his pranks, but upon going to the door saw to my utter astonishment an airship slowly descending upon my cow lot, about forty rods from the house...the ship had been gently descending until it was not more than thirty feet above the ground, and we came within fifty yards of it.

24

An electric airship of the era.
No relation whatsoever to aliens!

_____

It consisted of a great cigar-shaped portion, possibly three hundred feet long, with a carriage underneath.

The carriage was made of glass or some other transparent substance alternating with a narrow strip of some material.

It was brilliantly lighted within and everything was plainly visible-it was occupied by six of the strangest beings I ever saw.

They were jabbering together, but we could not understand a word they said.

Every part of the vessel which was not transparent was of dark reddish color. We stood mute with wonder and fright, when some noise attracted their attention and they turned a light directly upon us.

Immediately on catching sight of us they turned on some unknown power, and a great turbine wheel, about thirty feet in diameter, which was slowly revolving below the craft began to buzz and the vessel rose lightly as a bird.

When about three hundred feet above us it seemed to pause and hover directly over a two year old heifer, which was bawling and jumping, apparently fast in the fence.

Going to her, we found a cable  about a half inch in thickness made of some red material, fastened in a slip knot around her neck, one end passing up to the vessel, and the heifer tangled in the wire fence.

We tried to get it off but could not, so we cut the wire loose and stood in amazement to see the ship, heifer and all, rise slowly, disappearing in the northwest.

We went home, but I saw so frightened I could not sleep. Rising early Tuesday, I started out by horse, hoping to find some trace of my cow. This I failed to do, but coming back in the evening found that Link Thomas, about three or four miles west of Le Roy, had found the hide, legs and head in the field that day.

He, thinking someone had butchered a stolen beast, had brought the hide to town for identification, but was greatly mystified in not being able to find any tracks in the soft ground.

From the Chicago Eagle, May 9, 1896. Caption: "Dropping a torpedo from the clouds." At that time, nobody knew anything about those mysterious flying ships except of course, the engineers who built them in an absolute secrecy. Despite the enormous data and files on those "Dirigibles", many ancient astronauts, ancient aliens' theorists, and ufologists still believe that those crafts were extraterrestrial UFOS!!

Era's illustration of an airship.

After identifying the hide by my brand, I went home. But every time I would drop to sleep I would see the cursed thing, with its big lights and hideous people.

I don't know whether they are devils or angles, or what; but we all saw them, and my whole family saw the ship, and I don't want any more to do with them."

The Great Airship Scare ended in April 1897 with the last sighting of an airship over Yonkers, New York.

*** *** ***

**No aliens, and nothing extraterrestrial here!**
In conclusion, the airships were man-made, and had no relation whatsoever to extraterrestrials. They were built in Europe, and few were constructed in the United States, as documented by historical facts.

Many witnesses have reported that the airships made several landings, and their crew conversed with people, and asked for direction, supplies, and water for their crafts. The crews were polite, spoke in perfect English, and were dressed very normally; nothing to indicate that they were aliens. Some explained why they were flying those crafts, what their destination was, and where they came from.
The majority would say that they were exploring the countryside. Others were more discreet and didn't say much. Nevertheless, they were humans, and from the United States.
The bottom line is this: All those airships were the earliest types and categories of dirigibles, motor-driven, and crews-manned crafts, and had nothing to do with extraterrestrial UFOs.
Yet, ufologists still insist that they are of an extraterrestrial origin and piloted by aliens!

---

# Ufologists' false claims, accounts and explanations.

Ufologists have claimed that what people saw in the skies of 1896 and 1897 were extraterrestrial UFOs piloted by aliens. As usual they are wrong, and I am going to prove it to you. They argue that back then, no airship or any kind of a spacecraft was built, and/or was man-made in 1896 and 1897, simply because we did not have the technology of space-flight.

Little did they know that de facto in 1852, several types of crafts were built in Europe, and in 1894, 1895, 1896, and 1896, American entrepreneurs, businessmen and pilots began to build their own flying crafts, and kept them shrouded in secrecy, so competitors and business entrepreneurs would not know about it.

## Several types of crafts were built in Europe:

**In early 1852,** French Henry Giffard built the world first three-horse-power steam engine airship; a mechanical flying machine. And on September 24 of 1852, Giffard flew his craft from Paris to Trappes at an approximate speed of 8 kilometers per hour, covering an approximate distance of 27 kilometers.

**In 1853,** Sir George Cayley created the world's first airplanes' model and flew an airship at a speed of 6 kilometers per hour.

In fact, in 1809, Sir Cayley wrote mathematical formulae for space powered flights, and established technical data pertaining to drag and thrust.

**In 1872,** German flyer Paul Haenlein flew his airship at a higher speed and at a higher altitude, and took Europe by storm.

**In 1883,** French engineers and pilots Gaston Tissandier and Albert Tissandier built the world first flying machine powered by an electric engine "Moteur Electrique".

**In 1884,** French Charles Renard and Arthur Krebs built and flew "La France", an airship powered with an electric motor at an approximate speed of 23 kilometers per hour.

**In 1894,** Australian Lawrence Hargrave invented a motorized kite-plane which lifted a load of 208 pounds.

**In 1897,** German engineer David Schwartz built a revolutionary airship powered with a gasoline engine.

**In 1898,** Brazilian-French aristocrat Alberto Santos-Dumont flew a gasoline-powered dirigible, (round-trip) from Saint Cloud to the Eiffel Tower.

Santos-Dumont was the world's first pilot-entrepreneur to charter regular passengers' flights with his airship called No.9 dirigible.

Austrian German Otto Lillienthal (See below), nicknamed "The "Birdman of Berlin" had to his credits over 2,000 flights, but unfortunately his illustrious career ended in 1896 with a fatal crash.

Lawrence Hargrave on Australia's $20 bill.

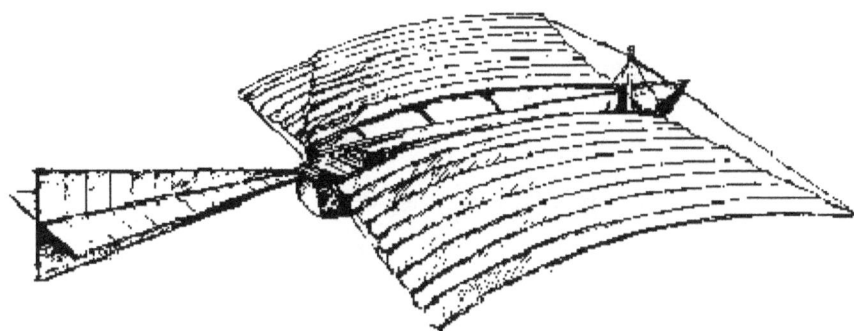

Sir George Cayley's first flying model, 1809.

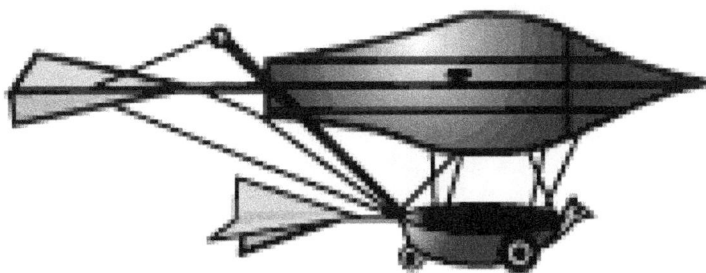

Sir George Cayley's first man-carrying glider, 1849.

Sir George Cayley's glider, 1848.

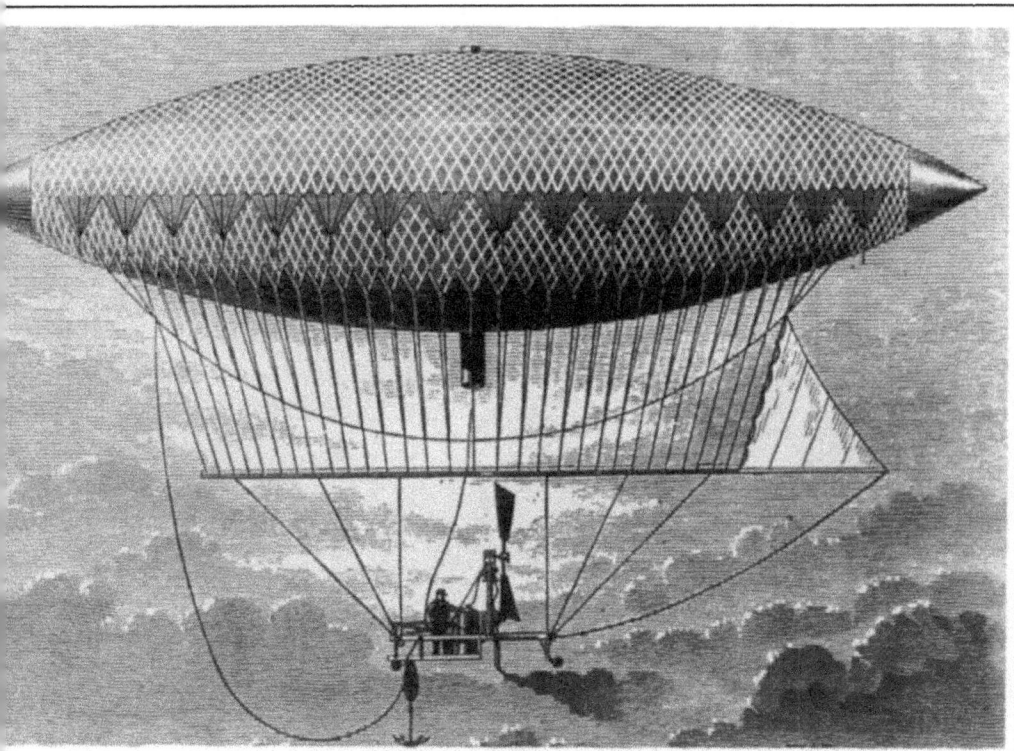

Henry Giffard's 144 foot long airship, launched on September 24, 1852.

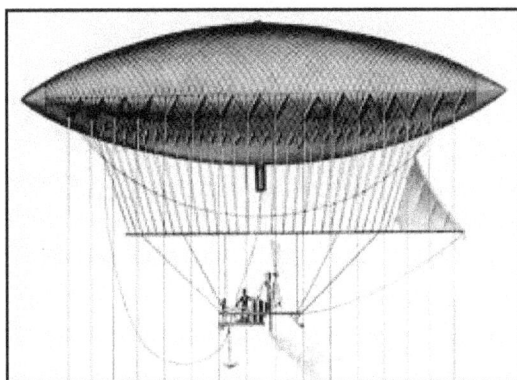

"La France" airship.

Arthur Krebs, co-builder of "La France" airship.

Alberto Santos-Dumont

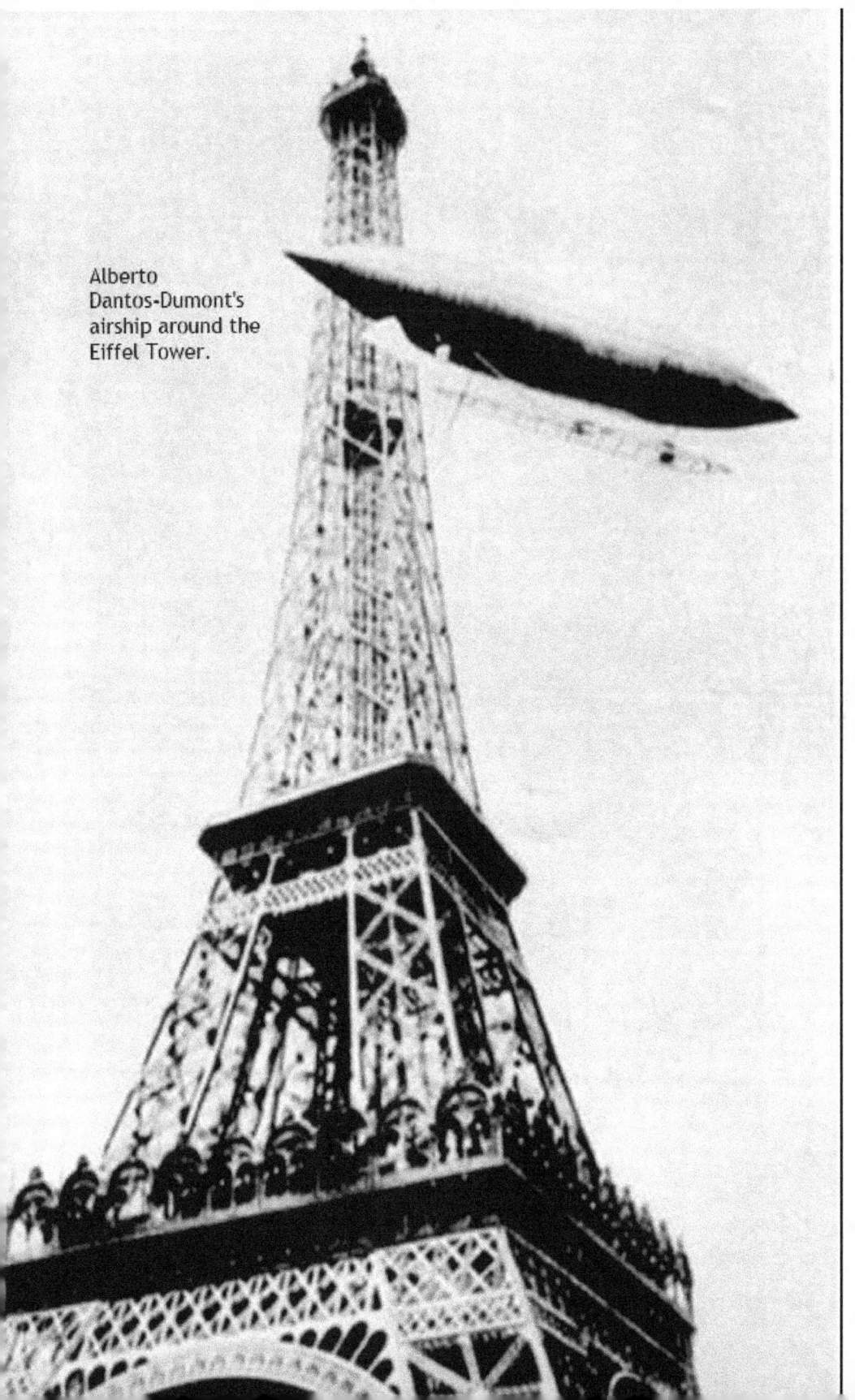

Alberto Dantos-Dumont's airship around the Eiffel Tower.

Alberto Dantos-Dumont's airship No. 9 over a French village.

Alberto Santos-Dumont dirigible airship.

French blueprints/patent of an airship design, 1852.

Count Ferdinand von Zeppelin's airship.

The ZR3

An all-metal airship built in 1897 by Serbian businessman and engineer David Schwarz, flew on November 3, 1897 over Berlin, Germany.

Engine of David Schwarz's airship.

Dr. H. Woelfert's airship, June 12, 1897, Germany.

Graf Zeppelin
mit dem Luftkreuzer „Z III" über Berlin

Original-Aufnahme 1909
Ø 1370/14

PHOTOCHEMIE, BERLIN

Zeppelin airship LZ III.

---

Various types of airships of the era.

---

## Several types of airships were built in the United States.
## American inventors and builders of airships:

---

Do not underestimate the American entrepreneurial spirit! During the American Civil War, Solomon Andrews built an airship and flew short distances.

- **In 1869,** British-American Frederick Marriott developed a model for transcontinental travel.
- **On July 2, 1869,** the 37-foot-long hydrogen filled balloon, "Avitor" powered with a steam engine and propellers mounted on its two wings flew, and became America's first controlled-flight aircraft.
- And at the San Francisco's Mechanics Fair, the "Avitor" flew 7 days a week, and transported thousands of spectators.

- **In 1889,** in Chicago, French-born Octave Chanute wrote "Progress in Flying Machines," which was considered back then as the world most authoritative aviation's technical reference and manual.
- **In 1891**, The Smithsonian Institution published "Experiments in Aerodynamics".
- **In 1895,** Cornell University granted Bachelor of Science degrees in aeronautics.
- **In 1895,** "The Aeronautical Annual" on flying machines was published.
- **On August 11, 1896,** Charles Abbot Smith received a patent number 565805 for his airship.
- **On April 20, 1897,** Henry Heintz received a patent number 580941 for his airship.
- **In 1896,** S.P. Langley flew two types of airships.
- **In 1896,** MIT began to offer courses in aeronautics and aviation, and MIT first degree in aeronautics was granted in 1892.
- **In 1896**, MIT built its first wind tunnel.

So, back then, in 1896 and 1897, we had the technology, the know-how, and the means that could have allowed us to fly. And there is no doubt that airships were built in America during those years.

But many pilots, inventors, businessmen, entrepreneurs and financiers of airplanes construction enterprises kept their inventions, airplanes and plans wrapped in secrecy for obvious reasons; business secrets and competition threats were two justifiable reasons for utmost secrecy.

\*\*\* \*\*\* \*\*\*

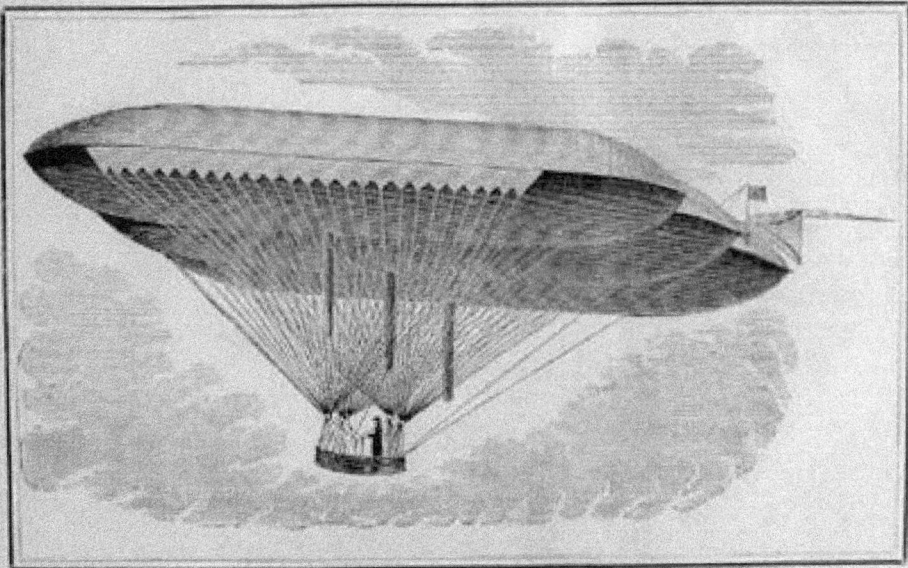

"Aereon", the First American dirigible "airship" built in 1863 by Solomon Andrews.

Octave Chanute

Solomon Andrews

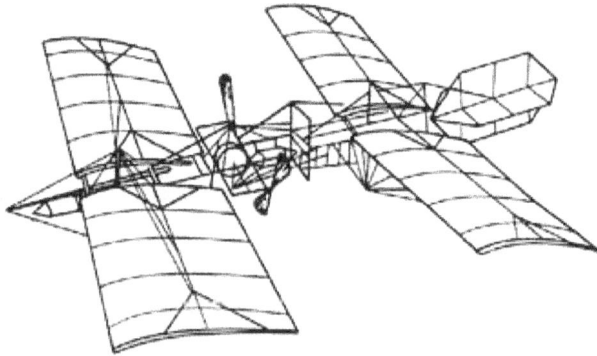

World's leading scientist in astrophysics, American Samuel Pierpoint Langley's steam-powered aeroplane.
It flew half of a mile, and was witnessed by Alexander Graham Bell.

# Recent Books by Maximillien de Lafayette

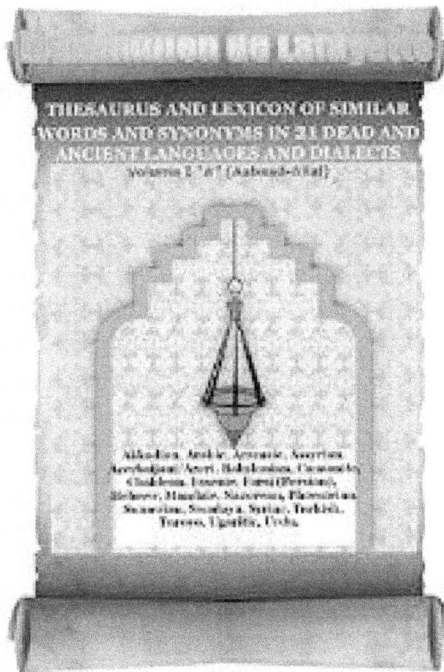

## THESAURUS AND LEXICON OF SIMILAR WORDS AND SYNONYMS IN 21 DEAD AND ANCIENT LANGUAGES AND DIALECTS

A set of 20 volumes. THESAURUS & LEXICON OF SIMILAR WORDS & SYNONYMS IN 21 DEAD & ANCIENT LANGUAGES AND DIALECTS.

Akkadian, Arabic, Aramaic, Assyrian, Azerbaijani/Azeri, Babylonian, Canaanite, Chaldean, Essenic, Farsi (Persian), Hebrew, Mandaic, Nazorean, Phoenician, Sumerian, Swadaya, Syriac, Turkish, Turoyo, Ugaritic, Urdu.

The world's 1st dictionary/thesaurus/lexicon of its kind! A gem. A literary treasure! Written by the world's most prolific linguist who authored 21 dictionaries of dead and ancient languages known to mankind. Published by Times Square Press NY.

**Maximillien de Lafayette**

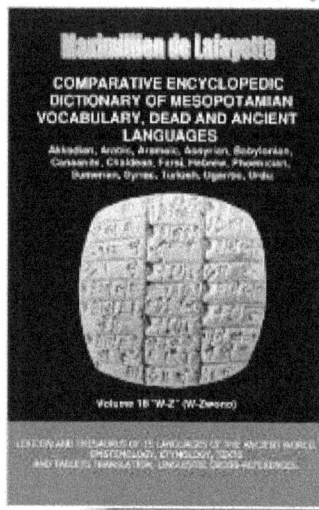

COMPARATIVE ENCYCLOPEDIC
DICTIONARY OF MESOPOTAMIAN
VOCABULARY, DEAD AND ANCIENT
LANGUAGES

Akkadian, Arabic, Aramaic, Assyrian, Babylonian,
Canaanite, Chaldean, Farsi, Hebrew, Phoenician,
Sumerian, Syriac, Turkish, Ugaritic, Urdu

Volume 18 "W-Z" (W-Zwosro)

LEXICON AND THESAURUS OF 15 LANGUAGES OF THE ANCIENT WORLD.
EPISTEMOLOGY, ETYMOLOGY, IDIOMS
AND TABLETS TRANSLATION, LINGUISTIC CROSS-REFERENCES.

**Comparative Encyclopedic Dictionary of
Mesopotamian Vocabulary, Dead and Ancient
Languages. Lexicon and Thesaurus of 15
Languages and Dialects of the Ancient World**
A set of 18 volumes (Approximately 4,200 pages).

---

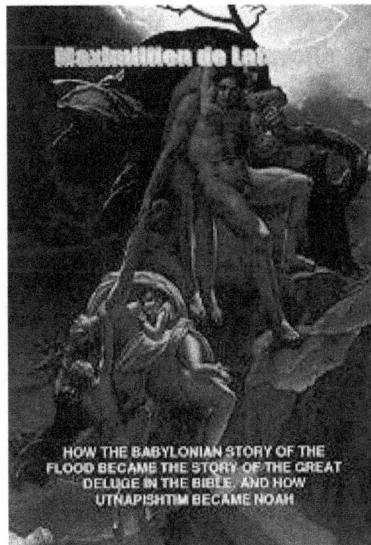

**How the Babylonian Story of the Flood Became the Story of the Great Deluge in the Bible. And How Utnapishtim Became Noah.**

From the content:
• Biblical stories taken from much older religions.
• The Babylonian Story of the Flood Versus the Biblical Story of the Flood.
• There is a difference of approximately 600 years between the Babylonian flood and the Biblical flood.
• Excerpts from the Mesopotamian texts, word-for-word, and my translation.
• Same stories in the Babylonian texts and the Bible:
• 1.The Anunnaki god Ea warned Utnapishtim about a flood.
• Instructions on how to build the boat.
• 2.Bringing animals to the boat.
• 3.The dove.
• 4.The birds are set free.
• 5.The boat resting on the top of a mountain.
• 6.Destroying mankind.

- 7.Reason for sending the flood.
- 8.Never again to bring a flood to earth and destroy mankind.
- 9.The 7th day of the flood.
- 10. Seven days of flood: In the Bible.
- 11.Waiting for the 7th day.
- 12.Sealing the door and cover of the boat with pitch.
- 13.Making a roof (Cover for the boat).
- 14.The covenant.
- 15.Offerings and sacrifices.
- 16.The blessing of Utnapishtim and Noah.
- Characteristics and dissimilarities of the three Babylonian versions of the story of the flood, the Epic of Gilgamesh and Berossus' account.
- The Sumerian story of the flood according to Berossus, a priest of the cult of Marduk in Babylon.

---

Don't Miss This Great Publication!

# Maximillien de Lafayette

## SCIENTIFIC AND ESOTERIC
## ENCYCLOPEDIA OF UFOS, ALIENS
## AND EXTRATERRESTRIALS GODS
### VOLUME I

The world's first, largest, most comprehensive and authoritative
publication of its kind. Everything you wanted to know about
aliens, extraterrestrials, Anunnaki, UFOs, secret black operations,
the origin and creation of mankind and religions.

## A SET OF 20 VOLUMES

Published by
Times Square Press
New York, Berlin
Website: www.timessquarepress.com

Printed in the
United States of America and Germany
2014

www.ingramcontent.com/pod-product-compliance
Lightning Source LLC
Chambersburg PA
CBHW022132280326
41933CB00007B/657